PREDATOR vs. PREY

HAWKS VS. RATTLESNAKES

FOOD CHAIN FIGHTS

SARAH ROGGIO

Lerner Publications ◆ Minneapolis

To my sister—my first artistic collaborator

Lerner Publications Company
An imprint of Lerner Publishing Group, Inc.
241 First Avenue North
Minneapolis, MN 55401 USA

For reading levels and more information, look up this title at www.lernerbooks.com.

Main body text set in Aptifer Sans LT Pro.
Typeface provided by Linotype AG.

Editor: Cole Nelson **Designer:** Kim Morales

Library of Congress Cataloging-in-Publication Data

Names: Roggio, Sarah, author.
Title: Hawks vs. rattlesnakes : food chain fights / Sarah Roggio.
Other titles: Hawks versus rattlesnakes
Description: Minneapolis : Lerner Publications, [2025] | Series: Predator vs. prey | Includes bibliographical references and index. | Audience: Ages 8–11 | Audience: Grades 4–6 | Summary: "Hawks and rattlesnakes are deadly creatures, but who would win in a fight? Readers can explore the strengths and weaknesses of each animal and learn how they survive in the wild"— Provided by publisher.
Identifiers: LCCN 2023039500 (print) | LCCN 2023039501 (ebook) | ISBN 9798765626757 (library binding) | ISBN 9798765629383 (paperback) | ISBN 9798765636206 (epub)
Subjects: LCSH: Red-tailed hawk—Juvenile literature. | Western diamondback rattlesnake—Juvenile literature. | Predation (Biology)—Juvenile literature. | Camouflage (Biology)—Juvenile literature. | Animal defenses—Juvenile literature. | Food chains (Ecology)—Juvenile literature.
Classification: LCC QL696.F32 R625 2025 (print) | LCC QL696.F32 (ebook) | DDC 597.96/38—dc23/eng/20231204

LC record available at https://lccn.loc.gov/2023039500
LC ebook record available at https://lccn.loc.gov/2023039501

Manufactured in the United States of America
1-1010122-52006-1/11/2024

TABLE OF CONTENTS

CHAPTER 1
DUEL IN THE DESERT 4

CHAPTER 2
RED-TAILED HAWK VS. WESTERN DIAMONDBACK RATTLESNAKE 8

CHAPTER 3
WHICH ANIMAL WILL WIN? 24

PREDATOR VS. PREY: HEAD-TO-HEAD 28

GLOSSARY 30

LEARN MORE 31

INDEX 32

CHAPTER 1

DUEL IN THE DESERT

IT'S HIGH NOON IN THE CHIHUAHUAN DESERT. The air is hot and dry. A western diamondback rattlesnake rests on the ground in the sun. Rattlesnakes are cold-blooded creatures. They need sunlight to keep their bodies warm.

Western diamondback rattlesnakes have black and white rings near their rattle.

Red-tailed hawks hunt from high perches.

Look out! A red-tailed hawk is perched nearby. It sinks its long talons into a Faxon yucca shrub. Hawks use these curved claws to snatch their prey. With its sharp eyes, the hawk spots the rattlesnake. It plans to make the rattlesnake its next meal.

A red-tailed hawk dives at its prey.

But this could be risky. Rattlesnakes are venomous reptiles. They use their fangs to poison prey and predators. The rattlesnake could kill the hawk with its bite.

The hawk swoops down and lands near the rattlesnake. The rattlesnake curls up its body into a tight coil of rings. Then it makes a loud, rattling sound by shaking its tail. It is warning the hawk to stay away. The hawk rises up on its strong feet and walks toward the rattlesnake. Will the hawk catch its prey? Let's find out!

RED-TAILED HAWK STATS

AVERAGE WINGSPAN: over 3.5 feet (1 m)

AVERAGE SPEED: 20 to 40 miles (32 to 64 km) per hour when soaring

SCARIEST SOUND: a loud screech that lasts two to three seconds

WESTERN DIAMONDBACK RATTLESNAKE STATS

AVERAGE BODY LENGTH: 4 to 6 feet (1.2 to 1.8 m)

AVERAGE SPEED: 6 to 10 feet (1.8 to 3 m) per second when striking its prey

SCARIEST SOUND: a loud rattle from shaking its tail up to ninety times per second

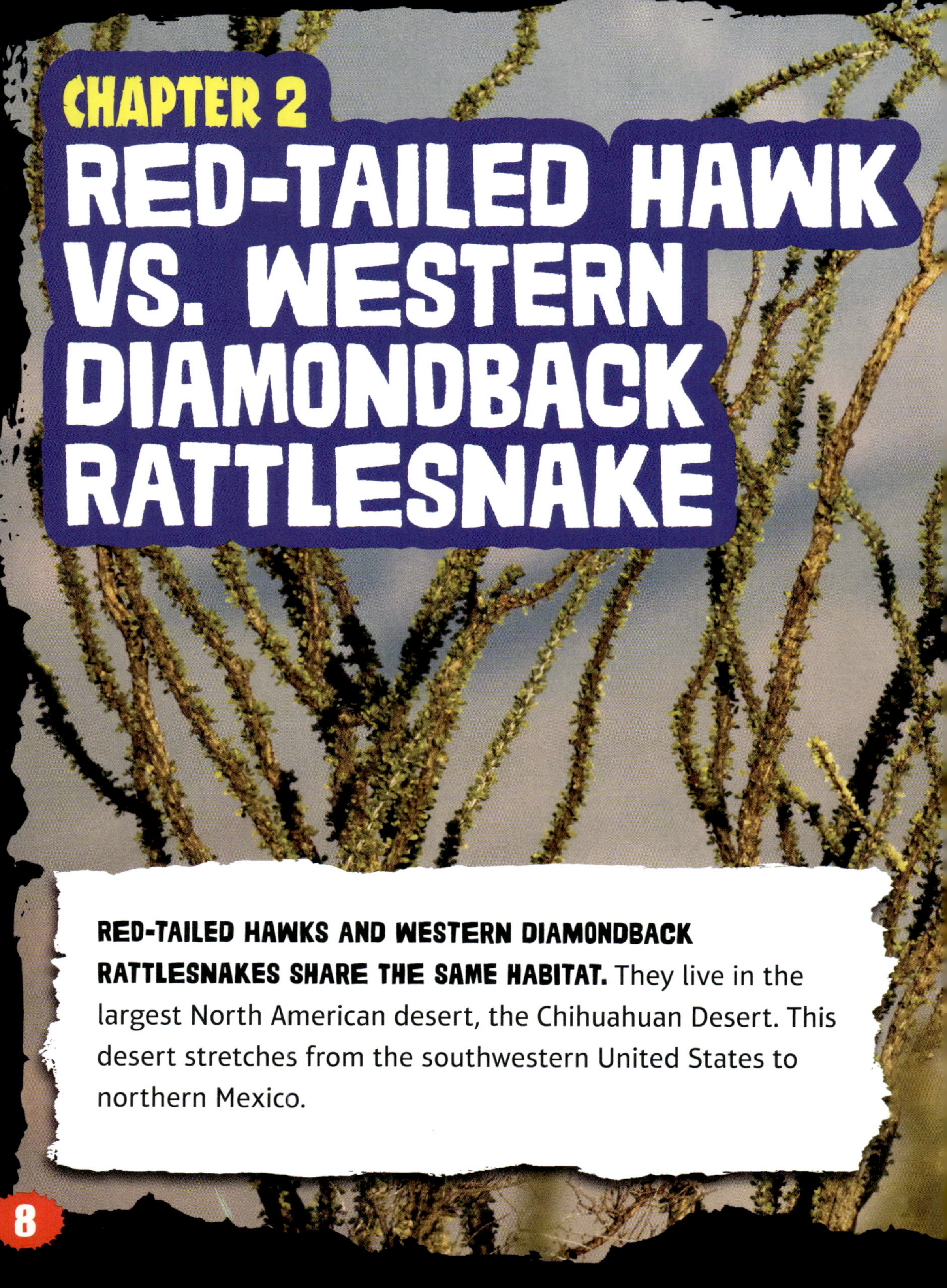

CHAPTER 2
RED-TAILED HAWK VS. WESTERN DIAMONDBACK RATTLESNAKE

RED-TAILED HAWKS AND WESTERN DIAMONDBACK RATTLESNAKES SHARE THE SAME HABITAT. They live in the largest North American desert, the Chihuahuan Desert. This desert stretches from the southwestern United States to northern Mexico.

Red-tailed hawks save energy by perching on branches or gliding in the air.

DIET AND HUNTING HABITS

Red-tailed hawks are carnivores. Their meals include snakes, squirrels, and other birds. They hunt alone during the day. They fight off other hawks that try to steal the food they catch. Over 250 hawk species live on all the continents except Antarctica. One of the biggest is the 2-foot-tall (0.6 m) ferruginous hawk. It hunts snakes, squirrels, and rabbits throughout North America.

Western diamondback rattlesnakes are also carnivores. They hunt alone at night. They can go weeks between meals. They eat birds, lizards, and mice. Rattlesnakes have heat-sensing pits near their nostrils. These pits help rattlesnakes find animals in the dark by sensing their warm bodies. These pits also give rattlesnakes their other name, pit vipers.

The world has over thirty rattlesnake species. Most dwell in North American deserts. For example, the northern black-tailed rattlesnake lives in the American southwest and northern Mexico. This rattlesnake climbs trees to warm up in the sun while hanging from lower branches.

A western diamondback rattlesnake shakes its rattle in warning.

Red-tailed hawks build nests high in the trees to raise their chicks.

SIZE

Red-tailed hawks are one of the biggest hawks in North America. They can grow up to 2 feet (0.6 m) tall. They make big, bowl-shaped nests in trees or on cliffs. Baby red-tailed hawks, or chicks, start out small but must be fed often. Their parents hunt to feed them.

Western diamondback rattlesnakes can grow up to 7 feet (2.1 m) long. The babies are only a foot (0.3 m) long, but they already have fangs and venom. They can defend themselves when their mother leaves right after they are born.

A hawk getting ready to catch its prey

STRENGTH

Red-tailed hawks have powerful talons. They use their talons to catch and kill their prey. A hawk's grip is three times stronger than a human's grip. Once these hawks sink their talons into prey, the prey can't escape.

SNEAKY HAWKS

Red-tailed hawks have a wingspan of over 3.5 feet (1 m). They fly high above when hunting their prey. Then they attack once their prey's guard is down.

THE BIGGEST RATTLESNAKE NEST IN THE WORLD

Mexico's Turtle Island has so many snakes that it's known as the biggest rattlesnake nest in the world. The island has a huge number of Tortuga (Turtle) Island rattlesnakes. Herpetologists, or snake scientists, go to Turtle Island to study its rattlesnakes.

Rattlesnakes have some of the quickest strikes and strongest bites of all snakes.

A western diamondback rattlesnake's bite is so strong that it can bite through a leather boot. These snakes also have flexible throats and jaws. When they eat animals, they open their jaws wide. Then they slide their mouths bit by bit around their meal. Rattlesnakes have the power to eat their prey whole. They can even swallow animals bigger than their own heads.

IS THAT A KITE?

Red-tailed hawks can use the wind to hold their bodies still when they're in the air to save energy. This is called kiting because they look like a kite when they do this.

A red-tailed hawk diving through the air

SPEED

Red-tailed hawks hunt by diving through the air toward their prey. They can dive as fast as 120 miles (193 km) per hour to catch animals on the ground. By the time the hawk's prey spots it, it's too late. The hawk has snatched it in its claws.

Western diamondback rattlesnakes strike their prey so fast that a human eye can't see it. The rattlesnake's fangs pump venom into its prey. Venom then kills the prey. The rattlesnake very slowly pulls the prey into its mouth after it's dead. The snake can spend over an hour swallowing a meal. It can take a snake days to digest its food.

A rattlesnake skipping over sand

SKIPPING OVER SAND

Sidewinder rattlesnakes move through the desert by skipping. They do this by throwing their bodies sideways in an S shape. This keeps part of their body off hot sand so they stay cool.

AGILITY

Red-tailed hawks have wide wings that are built to soar. They circle an area in the air while searching for prey. When male hawks want to find a mate, they dive to impress female hawks. The males may even play a daring game. They grab a female hawk's talons. Then they dive together toward the ground before pulling up at the last second.

Two red-tailed hawks prepare to dive together.

ACE FLYER

Cooper's hawks are built to hunt prey in the forest. Their round wings and long tail help steer them through the tangles of tree branches.

REGROWING TEETH

Sometimes a rattlesnake's fangs break off when it bites its prey. Rattlesnakes can regrow their fangs several times each year.

Western diamondback rattlesnakes have scales that help them blend into their habitat.

Western diamondback rattlesnakes mostly sneak up on animals in caves or on the ground. But they also swim or climb trees to pursue their prey.

WARNING SIGNS

Red-tailed hawks chase away other hawks that try to hunt near them. During mating season, male hawks screech at other hawks to defend their nesting spot.

A red-tailed hawk screeches in warning.

A western diamondback rattlesnake coiled and ready to strike

Rattlesnakes shake their rattles faster as predators get closer. Their rattles are made out of hard rings of keratin, the same material as human nails. These rings form each time a rattlesnake sheds its skin. The rattle sound comes from the keratin chunks clicking together.

Red-tailed hawks may eat larger meals on the ground.

KEY WEAPONS

Red-tailed hawks rely on long talons and sharp beaks to catch their prey. They carry small prey back to their perch to eat. These hawks also have sharp eyes. They can spot prey on the ground from 100 feet (30 m) up in the air.

Fangs and venom make western diamondback rattlesnakes quick killers. Their fangs inject venom that paralyzes an animal so it can no longer move. Then the venom kills that animal by poisoning its blood.

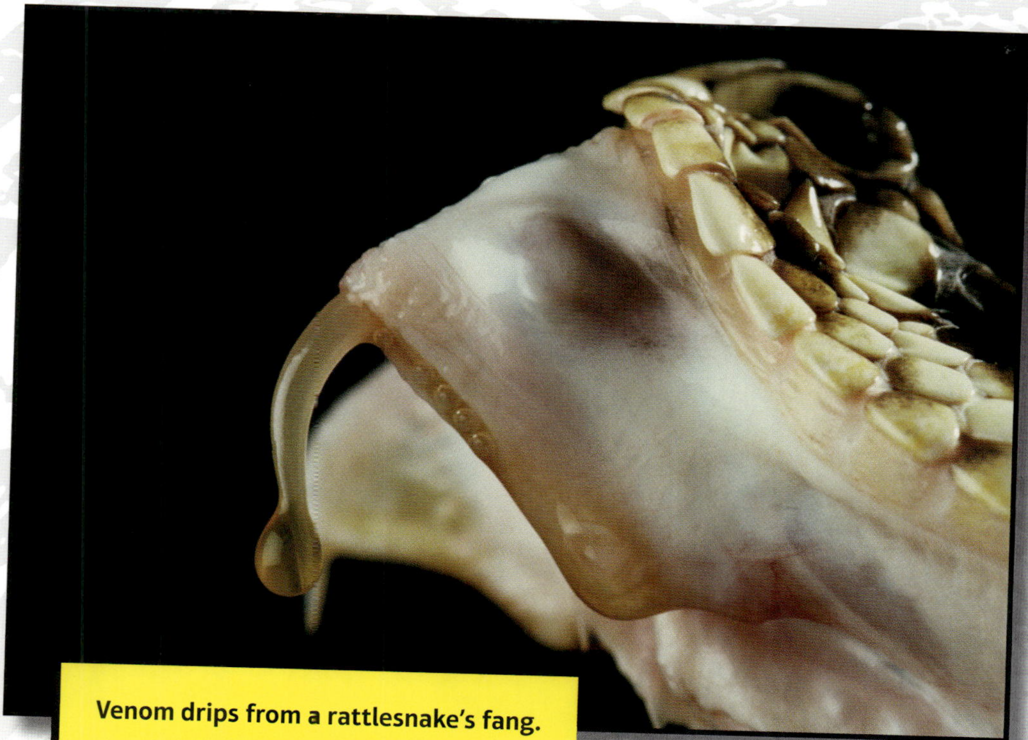

Venom drips from a rattlesnake's fang.

HIBERNATION

Western diamondback rattlesnakes spend their winters hibernating in caves. Hundreds of rattlesnakes will share the same cave in colder areas.

WEAKNESSES

Adult red-tailed hawks have few predators because they can escape quickly. Great-horned owls and crows will eat their eggs and chicks.

Some hawks have to build nests on buildings as human cities grow.

FEATHERED LEGS

The rough-legged hawk is covered in feathers from head to toe. The feathers help this hawk stay warm in its cold Arctic habitat.

Western diamondback rattlesnakes are cold-blooded creatures. This means they can't survive in extreme temperatures. They need some sun to keep their bodies warm. But they must hide under rocks or in caves if it's too hot. The diamond-shaped pattern on their bodies helps them blend in with desert rocks and dirt. They use this camouflage to hide from predators.

A western diamondback rattlesnake lies on sunny stones to keep its blood warm.

CHAPTER 3

WHICH ANIMAL WILL WIN?

THE HAWK IS CLOSING IN ON THE RATTLESNAKE. It holds its wings out wide as it walks. The hawk is trying to fool the rattlesnake into biting its wing feathers. That way the hawk will not get hurt if the rattlesnake strikes. But the rattlesnake turns quickly and wraps its body around the hawk's legs. If the rattlesnake can sneak in a bite, it could win this fight.

The rattlesnake tightens its grip. The hawk falls to the ground. The rattlesnake opens its mouth to bite. But the hawk strikes first with its sharp beak. Then the hawk spears the rattlesnake with its long talons. It tears into its meal.

A red-tailed hawk dives to catch its prey.

RULER OF THE HABITAT

Both rattlesnakes and hawks are at risk of losing their habitat because people are moving into areas where they live. But some red-tailed hawks are adapting to living in cities by building nests on bridges and buildings. Although rattlesnakes help control the number of mice and other rodents that people consider pests, some humans also hunt rattlesnakes.

A red-tailed hawk looks over its habitat.

A red-tailed hawk flies home with its catch.

Red-tailed hawks and rattlesnakes are both fast and dangerous predators. They take their time to hunt carefully. Rattlesnakes have venomous fangs that can take down most animals. But red-tailed hawks have two advantages over snakes: their sharp claws and beak!

Today the red-tailed hawk won the battle. The western diamondback rattlesnake fought back hard, but it could not escape the hawk's clutches. The hawk is the ruler of the desert.

PREDATOR VS. PREY: HEAD-TO-HEAD

RATTLESNAKE

- A tail rattles a warning to stay away.
- Venomous fangs poison prey.

RED-TAILED HAWK

- Circling helps search for prey.
- Sharp claws clutch and kill.

GLOSSARY

camouflage: physical features that help an animal blend in with its surroundings

carnivore: an animal that eats other animals

habitat: the place where a plant or animal naturally lives or grows

hibernate: a way for animals to survive the winter by resting and saving energy for long periods

keratin: the material that a snake's rattles and human nails are made of

predator: an animal that hunts other animals to eat

prey: an animal hunted by another animal for food

reptile: a cold-blooded animal, usually with scales, whose babies often hatch from eggs

species: a group of animals that are all the same type

venom: poison that an animal passes to prey through a bite or sting

LEARN MORE

Flood, Joe. *Birds of Prey: Terrifying Talons*. New York: First Second, 2022.

Hubbard, Ben. *Lions vs. Zebras: Food Chain Fights.* Minneapolis: Lerner Publications, 2025.

Kiddle: Hawk Facts for Kids
https://kids.kiddle.co/Hawk

Musgrave, Ruth. *Poisonous and Venomous Animals*. New York: DK, 2023.

National Geographic Kids: Rattlesnake
https://kids.nationalgeographic.com/animals/reptiles/facts/rattlesnake

National Geographic Kids: Red-Tailed Hawk
https://kids.nationalgeographic.com/animals/birds/facts/red-tailed-hawk

INDEX

beaks, 20, 24, 27

carnivore, 9–10
Chihuahuan Desert, 4, 8
cold-blooded, 23

fangs, 6, 11, 15, 21, 27
feathers, 24

hunting, 9–11, 14, 18, 26–27

predators, 6, 19, 22–23, 27
prey, 5–6, 12–17

rattles, 19

tail, 6
talons, 5, 12, 16, 20, 24

venom, 6, 11, 15, 21, 27

PHOTO ACKNOWLEDGMENTS

Image credits: Dennis W Donohue/Shutterstock, p. 4; franzfoto.com/Alamy, p. 5; David Brace/Shutterstock, pp. 6, 29; rck_953/Shutterstock, p. 7 (top); Chase D'animulls/Shutterstock, p. 7 (bottom); Rolf Nussbaumer Photography/Alamy, pp. 8–9; Stan Tekiela Author/Naturalist/Wildlife Photographer/Getty Images, p. 10; Breck P. Kent/Shutterstock, p. 11; Ronnie Howard/Shutterstock, p. 12; Audrey Snider-Bell/Shutterstock, p. 13; Chris McNeill/Getty Images, p. 14; Nature Picture Library/Alamy, p. 15; Andrew Breslow/Getty Images, p. 16; jokerbethyname/Shutterstock, p. 17; Randy Fuchs/Shutterstock, p. 18; Thomas Torget/Shutterstock, p. 19; Daniel Friend/Shutterstock, p. 20; robertharding/Alamy, p. 21; Science History Images/Alamy, p. 22; Andrew DuBois/Alamy, p. 23; Tom Reichner/Shutterstock, p. 24; Rob Palmer Photography/Shutterstock, p. 25; Sam Carrera/Shutterstock, p. 26; David Wheat/Shutterstock, p. 27; Audrey Snider-Bell/Shutterstock, p. 28. Design elements: iunewind/Shutterstock; Milano M/Shutterstock; Ukrainian studio/Shutterstock; Cassel/Shutterstock; Textures and backgrounds/Shutterstock; Print Net/Shutterstock.

Cover: Jordan Confino/Getty Images; Mary Ann McDonald/Getty Images.